theimaginary**body**

presents

100

created by
diene petterle
and christopher heimann

written by
neil monaghan,
diene petterle
and christopher heimann

devised by
the company

The 2003 run at the Soho Theatre in London
and subsequent national and international tours
are presented by **the**imaginary**body** in association with
Glynis Henderson Productions Ltd.

100

*was originally produced by **the**imaginary**body** and received its world premiere at the Smirnoff Underbelly on 1 August 2002 during the Edinburgh Festival.*

Matt Boatright-Simon	ALEX
Matthieu Leloup	KETU
Tanya Munday	SOPHIE
Claire Porter	NIA
Lawrence Werber	GUIDE

Neil Monaghan	*co-writer*
Christopher Heimann	*director and co-writer*
Diene Petterle	*producer and co-writer*
Adam Crosthwaite	*lighting designer*
Soutra Gilmour	*set designer*
Annemarie Woods	*costume designer*
Matthieu Leloup	*movement work*
Steve King	*associate producer*
Hannele Brown	*associate producer*

John Hickman and Thomas Gurney	*web designers*
Nevil Mountford	*photographer*
Christoph Stolberg	*corporate design*

A work in progress version of *100* was presented at the Arcola Theatre in London in August 2001, performed by Syan Blake, Annabel Capper, Matthieu Leloup, Ita O'Brien and Kosh Omar. Lighting design by Sven Ortel, set/costume design by Margarita Juan. Creative collaborator: Penny Cliff.

Our collaborators along the way

Ruth Baldwin, Anil Desai, Alma Fridell, Maggie O'Brien,
William Rowsey, Gal Sapir, Christina Thanasoula

Thanks to

Sue Emmas and everyone at the Young Vic Theatre
Mehmet Ergen and everyone at the Arcola Theatre
Richard Lee and everyone at the Jerwood Space
Rebecca Salt at Colman Getty PR

Special thanks to

Markolf Heimann, Christine Heimann-Bossert,
Diethard Heimann, Hedwig Bossert, Reinhard Bestgen,
Ruy Petterle, Hans and Carolyn Kohl, Manuela Maiguashca,
Zoe Hassid, Susanna Bauer and Zia Trench

For further information, photographs and interviews
please contact Glynis Henderson Productions Ltd
on info@ghmp.co.uk, tel +44 (0) 20 7580 9644
and fax +44 (0) 20 7436 1489

BIOGRAPHIES

Christopher Heimann – *director and co-writer*

Co-wrote and directed *100* in a devising process at the Young Vic and Arcola Theatres, London. Christopher directed a video installation for *Mincemeat* by Cardboard Citizens ('remarkable . . . multi-layered, passionate and as innovative as anything on the London stage' – Lyn Gardner, The Guardian), *Bold Girls* at the Hens and Chicken's, London ('emotionally charged production . . . tight direction that does justice to the award-winning play' – Time Out) and *Las Cosas Tienen Vida* at the Tribal Theater, Spain. He has also directed two short films for the Gate Theatre, and one documentary for the Big Issue Foundation, screened at the Lux Centre and Britart.Com for a month for the Big Issue's tenth anniversary celebrations. He directed the Michael Chekhov Training Programme for professional actors for two years, and has been a workshop director at the Gate Theatre, the Young Vic, the Arcola Theatre, Stratford Circus and for Orange Communications. Originally from Germany, Christopher trained as an architect at first, and then as an actor at Cygnet Training Theatre (patron Peter Brook).

Diene Petterle – *co-writer and producer*

Diene Petterle co-wrote and produced *100*. She is an award-winning writer/director of character-driven films. Her latest short film, *Mr Thompson's Carnation*, was premiered at Cannes 2001, won the Short Circuits Award and was subsequently theatrically released in front of a feature film in London (Richmond Filmhouse). It has been touring the world in the international festival circuit and was lately screened at the 46th Regus London Intl. Film Festival. It has been selected by the British Council to represent the UK abroad for the next two years, showcasing the quality of British filmmaking around the world, incl. Germany, Brazil, Ukraine and Austria. It is also being distributed worldwide by Britshorts having been broadcast in Spain, Portugal, Andorra and Australia ('A film that carries the sort of achingly sad kick that lingers for hours' (Hot Dog, the award-winning cinema magazine, March 2002).

Her other fictional work as a writer/director includes the short films *Fardo, Fate* (Portuguese Kodak Award), *Racing Rats* and *The Issue of the Case*. Originally from Brazil, Diene has a degree in TV Production and an MA in Film Directing.

Neil Monaghan – *co-writer*

Writing credits include the critically acclaimed *Beautiful People*, commissioned by Alan Ayckbourn for the Stephen Joseph Theatre, Scarborough, and the controversial play *Eye Contact*, starring Kelly

Brook, which was a box office smash for the Riverside Studios, London. His other theatre work includes *Dot Com* and *Bolt from the Blue* (both for Stephen Joseph Theatre Scarborough). *Dot Com* was also adapted for radio and broadcast on Radio 4. Shows at the Edinburgh Festival between 1992 and 1998 include *The Good Fight*, *Under Glass*, *The Bloody Chamber*, *The Cenci* and *Burnout*. Television credits include *Life's Too Short*, a sitcom commissioned by the BBC, and *Bella Donna*, a comedy drama series for Granada TV. Film credits include *Human Nature* and *After Image*. Neil also wrote and took photographs for John Prescott's battle bus campaign diary during the 2001 general election.

Adam Crosthwaite – *lighting design*

Recent work includes *South of the River* for the ENO Baylis Programme, *Shirley Valentine* at the Palace Theatre Westcliff, *The Yellow Wallpaper* for Strathcona Theatre Company, *The Shout* at the Drill Hall, *Twelfth Night* at the Cambridge Arts Theatre, *L'Elisir D'Amore* for New Sussex Opera, *While I Was Waiting* and *Damned and Divine* for the ENO Studio, *Dialogues des Carmelites* at the Edinburgh Festival Theatre, *Peer Gynt* at the Battersea Arts Centre, and *Glass Hearts*, *Creditors* and *Pariah* at Southwark Playhouse. Other lighting designs include *The Odyssey* at the Gate Theatre, ('Adam Crosthwaite's superb lighting accomplishes subtle shifts of mood and location' – Evening Standard) and shows at Hampstead Theatre and the Whitehall Theatre. Overseas work includes *Tosca* and *The Barber of Seville* for the Manoel Theatre, Malta, and *Hawking's Dream* at the Kunstlerhaus Theatre, Vienna.

Soutra Gilmour – *set design*

Soutra has designed a wide variety of work in theatre, opera and film. Theatre includes: *Peer Pan* at Tramway, Glasgow, *Antigone* at Citizens Theatre, Glasgow, *The Birthday Party* at Sheffield Crucible, *Fool for Love* for The English Touring Company, *Hand in Hand* (Hampstead Theatre), *Shadow of a Boy* (National Theatre) and five productions at the Gate Theatre, London. Opera includes: *El Cimarron* at Queen Elizabeth Hall, Southbank, *Bathtime* (English National Opera Studio) and *A Better Place* (English National Opera, London Coliseum).

Annemarie Woods – *costume design*

Annemarie studied set and costume design at Wimbledon School of Art. She has designed for both theatre and film. Her most recent work includes costume and set design for *You Hang Up First* (Contact Theatre, Manchester, directed by Dana Fainaru). She is currently assisting Gideon Davey on *The Ring Cycle* for the Bayerische Staatsoper.

CAST

Matt Boatright-Simon: – *Alex*

Theatre acting work includes Prospero in *Prospero's Island*, *Sexual Perversity in Chicago* (Garage Theatre, London), the role of Tybalt in *Romeo and Juliet* (LA Theatre Centre, LA), and *Letters Home* (Stella Adler Theatre, LA ('Matt Boatright-Simon overwhelms the stage with a relaxed confidence' – Variety). Screen and TV credits include *Beverly Hills 90210* and the pimp in *How The Pimp Saved Christmas* (Behemoth films). Matt is originally from the USA.

Matthieu Leloup – *Ketu*

Matthieu has collaborated with the**imaginary**body since its creation and is part of the original cast of *100* at the Arcola and in Edinburgh. He has trained in Ecole Jacques Lecoq (Paris) and Theatre D-Nue (Paris), in England, and at Judith Holzer's Movement Laboratory in Java and Bali. He has founded and directed Tribal Theater (Spain), was visiting director for Bilbo dance Company in Paris, and artistic director of Les Hordes ETO company in Paris. He is currently artist in residence with Song of the Goat Theatre, Wroclaw, Poland, and collaborating with ZIMT Company as a director. Theatre includes: *Romeo and Juliet*, *Christmas Carol* (Cygnet Theatre, patron Peter Brook, Exeter); *Cosas tienen vida propria* (Tribal Theatre); *Le Songe de Basile* (Bilbo), Brecht's *Fear and Misery of the Third Reich*, *Cet Animal Etrange* (Theatre D-Nue)

Tanya Munday – *Sophie*

Tanya trained at RADA. Theatre includes: *Woyzeck* (Theatre Melange, National Tour), *The White Devil* (Galleon Productions, Greenwich Playhouse), *Andorra* (Greg Thompson, The Young Vic), *Larte della Commedia* (Clive Mendus, The Old Vic), *Mountain Language* (Katie Mitchell, The Royal Court) and *Fxxx The State* (Hungry Horse Productions, The Pleasance, Edinburgh Festival). Professional Workshops include: National Theatre Studio, Shared Experience, Derevo, Theatre Melange and Trestle Theatre Company. TV credits include *Casualty*, *Eastenders* and *The Bill*.

Claire Porter – *Nia*

For the last three years Claire has played Miss Drill in Jill Murphy's The *Worst Witch* for ITV. Previous theatre work includes: the original production of *100* at the Edinburgh Festival, 2002; *Lady Windermere's Fan* at the Theatre Royal, Haymarket, and The Royal Exchange, Manchester; Mark Rylance's *The Tempest* at The Globe Theatre; Beth in *The Drowning Point* and Sarah in *The Lover* for Blue Green Productions; Maddie in *Between the Gods and the Gutter; Medea, Sansovino's Island* and *Three Dolls Called Daisy* for Paines Plough Theatre Company. Other Television and film work includes: *One Foot in the Algarve, The House of Eliott* and *The Little Matchmaker* for the BBC, *Space Invaders* for Strauss Films.

Lawrence Werber – *Guide*

Theatre acting work includes *The Merchant of Venice* (dir. Trevor Nunn, Royal National Theatre), *Countrymania* (dir. Mike Alfreds, Royal National Theatre), *The Merchant of Venice* (dir. Peter Hall, starring Dustin Hoffman, Phoenix Theatre), *The Ends of the Earth* (Royal National Theatre), *The Miser* (dir. Mike Alfreds, Oxford Stage Company), *Punishment Without Revenge* (Actors Touring Company), *The Grapes of Wrath* (Birmingham Rep), *The Flight Into Egypt* (Hampstead Theatre), *Shrew'd* (Arcola Theatre), and *Pariah* (Southwark Playhouse). Film and TV credits include *Casualty, The Bill, Secret Weapon, Simon Magus, To Play the King, Trial and Retribution*, and *Fist of Fun*.

theimaginarybody

is interested in creating narrative-driven drama with a focus on visual styles that reflect content in innovative ways, both in theatre and film. Its Artistic Directors are acclaimed German theatre director Christopher Heimann and award-winning Brazilian film-maker Diene Petterle. Both have been developing work that toys with magical realism, trying to stretch boundaries between reality and fiction. Christopher and Diene met at the Gate Theatre in London, where they co-directed films made by homeless people.

As an international company, **the**imaginary**body** collaborates with actors from diverse backgrounds. The fusion of different theatrical influences (including Michael Chekhov and Lecoq) informs the company's approach to the work.

theimaginary**body**'s body of work includes the short film *Mr. Thompson's Carnation*, which was premiered at Cannes 2001, won the Short Circuits Award and was subsequently theatrically released in front of a feature film at the Richmond Filmhouse in London. It has been touring the world in the international film festival circuit and was lately screened at the 46th Regus London International Film Festival at the National Film Theatre. The British Council selected the film to represent the United Kingdom abroad for two years, showcasing the quality of British filmmaking. Consequently it has been screened in cinemas and festivals in Germany, Brazil, Austria, Ukraine and Australia. Having secured world-wide distribution by Britshorts, the film has been broadcast in Spain, Portugal, Andorra and Australia. The award-winning cinema magazine Hot Dog describes it: *'A film that carries the sort of achingly sad kick that lingers for hours.'* *Mr. Thompson's Carnation* was written and directed by Diene Petterle and produced by Manuela Maiguashca.

theimaginary**body** has also run workshops in a wide range of settings. Professional theatres include the Young Vic Theatre, the Arcola Theatre and the Gate Theatre. Community work includes the Big Issue Foundation and educational work includes Brunel University.

www.theimaginarybody.co.uk
info@theimaginarybody.co.uk

Glynis Henderson Productions Ltd

produces, general manages and represents a variety of theatre, music and dance productions. The company specialises in introducing unique and exciting new work to an international audience.

GHP is the original co-producer of *Stomp* along with the show's creators Yes/No Productions, and has co-produced *Stomp* worldwide (with the exception of North America) for 10 years. *Stomp* has toured to over 40 countries and GHP is currently presenting the show at the Vaudeville Theatre in London and on a major tour throughout Europe, Eastern Europe and Scandinavia in association with Yes/No Productions. Amongst other awards STOMP won a Laurence Olivier Award for Best Choreography and was nominated for a Laurence Olivier Award for Best Entertainment.

GHP has managed and produced Ennio Marchetto for over ten years. Ennio, the living cartoon, was nominated for The Drama Desk Award for Unique Entertainment and The Laurence Olivier Award for Best Entertainment. Ennio continues to tour world-wide and has performed in over 50 countries including recent seasons in New York, San Francisco, Los Angeles, Barcelona, Japan and on tour throughout the UK. Ennio opens in Toronto in December 2002.

GHP has also managed and produced theatre O since 2000, when *Three Dark Tales* caused a sensation at the Edinburgh Festival. *Three Dark Tales* has since toured to Australia, New Zealand, Brazil and Sweden and GHP co-produced a New York season. The show will tour to China later this year. Theatre O are creating a new play, *The Argument*, which will tour the UK and then play the Edinburgh Festival 2003 and BITE:03 at the Barbican Theatre. In addition, GHP is producing its third UK tour of the Wadaiko Yamato Drummers of Japan in 2003.

Shows currently being developed by GHP Ltd include *On Earth* (*as it is*) with Andrew Wale and Perrin Manzer Allen (the creators of Jacques Brel's *Anonymous Society* – TMA Best Musical Award). *On Earth* (*as it is*) will premiere at the Edinburgh Festival in 2003.

GHP in association with CanStage will be producing *The Overcoat* (originally conceived and directed by Morris Panych and Wendy Gorling) at BITE:04 at the Barbican Theatre.

Past productions and tours include: *Eddie Izzard in Paris*, *Rich Fulcher's Mom*, *I'm Not A Lawyer*, *Cool Heat Urban Heat*, *The Harlem Gospel Singers*, *The Mapapa Acrobats*, *Paul Morocco's Ole*, *Modern Problems in Science*, Ardal O'Hanlon, Odense Internationale Musikteater's *Lulu* and *MacHomer*.

● soho
● theatre + writers' centre

The Soho Theatre Development Campaign

Soho Theatre Company receives core funding from Westminster City Council and London Arts. And additional support by donations from trusts, foundations and individuals and corporate involvement.

Gordon's

Bloomberg

TBWA\GGT DIRECT

Our major sponsors are committed to developing the arts and with the assistance of Arts and Business New Partners encouraging a creative partnership with the sponsors and their employees. This translates into special ticket offers, creative writing workshops, innovative PR campaigns and hospitality events.

A&B
Arts & Business
NEW PARTNERS

In 1996, Soho Theatre Company was awarded an £8 million Lottery grant from the Arts Council of England to help create the Soho Theatre + Writers' Centre. An additional £2.6 million in matching funds was raised and over 500 donors supported the capital appeal. The full list of supporters is displayed on our website at www.sohotheatre.com/thanks.htm

Soho Theatre and Writers' Centre
21 Dean St, London W1D 3NE

Admin: 020 7287 5060 *Fax:* 020 7287 5061 *Box Office:* 020 7478 0100
www.sohotheatre.com
Registered Charity: 267234

100

Created by Diene Petterle and Christopher Heimann

Written by Neil Monaghan, Diene Petterle
and Christopher Heimann

Devised by **the**imaginary**body** theatre company

Introduction

Our journey – an unusual process

The work on *100* started with an email from the Arcola theatre in London, in July 2001. It offered Diene and me the opportunity to put on a play as part of the theatre's Short Cuts season of short plays – the only condition was that the piece had to be ready exactly one month later.

Instead of looking for a play, we felt we were more interested in creating a play based on certain themes we felt strongly about. As we sat down and brainstormed, a number of starting points appeared:

One was the question of what may be essential in life. We wondered what it would be like to stop, step out, look at our lives and reconsider our choices. We had often felt that we, as most Londoners, were running around and missing some kind of balance in our everyday lives. How would we be living our lives if we had a clear sense of what was essential, what was really important to us?

The theme of death and dying had been of interest to both of us, for different reasons. And it also seemed to follow on naturally from the previous point: isn't death the ultimate 'stop'? One often hears stories of how 'near-death experiences' make people completely re-evaluate their lives and often make changes for the better. Why do we need to almost die to ask ourselves these questions? And can't the idea of Judgment Day or Purgatory be understood in a similar way, as an instance that poses the very same questions?

Another starting point was our shared love for the literary style of Magical Realism and the work of Gabriel Garcia Marquez in particular. We were inspired by the way in which reality and fantasy blend seamlessly in his novels. We also knew that while dealing with serious issues, we really wanted to bring a magical sense of wonder, lightness and fun into our piece. In fact, some of the memories in the play have been inspired by Marquez' novel *One Hundred Years Of Solitude*.

Out of these starting points we created the premise and narrative structure for *100*, and outlines of characters and character journeys.

What followed was a period of ten intense days in a rehearsal room, improvising with a group of actors. All the collaborators contributed immensely.

At the end of these ten days, and exactly one month after the initial email, we presented *100* at the Arcola theatre as a work-in-progress piece on three evenings. We felt we had found the core of something that was very special and dear to us. The audience response was very strong and positive, too. We decided to develop *100* and take it to the Edinburgh Festival.

While the heart of the piece was already well developed at this infancy stage, we were very much aware that we needed to fundamentally rework the piece. We felt that while the devising process was very creative, we weren't sure it would lead us to the quality of dialogue and clarity of shape we were looking for, especially given the limited amount of time we were able to have with actors in the rehearsal room.

Diene and I were also aware that we were not the right people to do this work alone, as we are both not native English speakers. So we began to look for a scriptwriter to collaborate with. This turned out to be a lot more difficult than expected. Over the following months we searched, while we also went through another period of script development and improvisations with a group of actors at the Young Vic theatre in London.

Finally – and with the help of the internet – our path and Neil's met. Together, we tried to go back to the essence of the piece. Over the following months in the run up to the Edinburgh Festival, Neil wrote several drafts from scratch.

These drafts went back and forth between him, Diene and myself, being constantly reworked and developed. Our collaboration was getting more and more fruitful and it soon became clear that we had become a new creative team, a team of three. We were complete.

On the first day of rehearsal, four weeks before the Edinburgh Festival, it became apparent that our script wasn't ready enough to be the basis of the rehearsal process. The script at this point reflected a very fertile ground with intriguing possibilities but it was far from a finished product. We decided to go back to creating a very detailed precise narrative outline of the play. Based on this outline we started a parallel process of improvising in the rehearsal room while writing the play simultaneously, with both processes feeding off and into each other. Our new company of actors were seasoned improvisers and their creative juices were just what *100* needed to fulfil its potential. Their flexibility, generosity and calm support kept the boat afloat. Matthieu Leloup ran daily sessions of movement work, creating a great sense of ensemble and alertness in the company, which informed the improvisation process. Having been involved with *100* since the very beginning, his contribution inside and outside the rehearsal room was a defining influence to the piece.

It was in this period that our unusual writers' collaboration became most intense and probably most creative. It felt like all three of us were constantly pushing each other further and surprising each other. At some point we even had the ocean as an obstacle, as Neil went on a holiday he'd planned long before *100,* only to realise he was to spend most of his time in Chicago on a borrowed computer, adapting the results from my improvisations in the rehearsal room and Diene's narrative structure development in the office. Gradually all the elements came together until final adjustments to the play were being made in the car driving up to Edinburgh (two days before we opened!)

At the Edinburgh Festival, the play sold out even before the reviews came out and won a *Fringe First* award for 'innovation in theatre and outstanding new production at the 2002 Edinburgh Festival'. The entire creative period had been an incredibly vibrant, inspiring, intense and utterly exhausting process and at the time of writing, we're about to embark on an extensive international and national tour – ready to start it all over again . . .

(This published version of 100 has been slightly reworked since Edinburgh).

Notes on the production

The setting of 100 is a fluid interchange between a magical void space between life and death where the characters struggle to choose, and the worlds inside their memories.

One of our starting points for this production was the question of what exactly is this idea called 'the magic of theatre'.

I now think the magic lies in the fact that as an audience we can believe in something that we know isn't true. The moments of magic are the ones where we see a character, space or object suddenly transform into something else, purely through the actor's craft playing with our imagination – while to the eye, 'in reality', nothing much has really changed.

The simultaneous existence of these two (contrasting) worlds, ie. the meeting of actors and audience here and now, and the belief of the audience in the created imaginary world, is what may constitute the unique feature of theatre.

So I decided to explore this 'magic of theatre' through creating a flow of transformation of objects, characters and the space by the simplest means. How little do we need to suggest for images to appear in the audience's inner eye?

Once again going back to the theme of what is essential (this time in theatre, rather than in life) I set myself a certain parameter: to make a show using only bamboo sticks. All the effects of the play were to be created only by the actors (supported by lighting), without any scenery or props other than the sticks . . . and one orange.

Consequently, whenever a character in the play begins to recall his or her memory, the other actors transform with bamboo sticks into the scenery and characters of this memory.

For example: as Ketu begins to recall his memory, the lights slowly fade up around him. In a bright warm morning light, we see the other actors as trees holding the bamboo sticks like dangling vines. The image of a rainforest is evoked through the use of the bamboos, together with a soundscape that the actors create with their voices. Ketu enters the image and as he uses his stick as a paddle, the trees begin to advance upstage in his direction, in sync with the rhythm of his paddle movement. He is travelling on the Amazon! As he passes through the trees, ie. as the trees move upstage of him, they transform with a single movement from trees with vines into characters with paddles. Instantaneously the space transforms and we now see a group of natives in boats, within the forest as a backdrop that has already been established in our imagination.

The worlds we create are as fragile – and beautiful – as soap bubbles: one wrong movement, one actor who is not fully connected with the image and the bubble bursts, leaving us only with an actor holding a stick. The demands of this work – its need for mutual awareness and co-operation, for care and humility – are in themselves crucial to the meaning of the piece.

CHRISTOPHER HEIMANN

Characters

in order of appearance

KETU

SOPHIE

ALEX

GUIDE

NIA

Although the play was originally performed by a cast of five, it could be played by a larger cast.

Within the 'memory scenes' the performers help to act out episodes from each other's lives, transforming into characters and objects as necessary.

Void

The lights fade up from black. We are in a seemingly vast space, largely empty and without recognisable dimensions. Light floods in from an unknown source. This is the Void, an otherworldly place, perhaps outside time and space. The stage area contains four, apparently randomly placed, boxes.

After a few seconds we become aware of movement.

KETU appears, like a shadow in the outermost edge of the space. Apparently in his mid to late thirties, his movements have something distinctly animal about them. He is clearly confused and disorientated.

Then SOPHIE appears, a woman in her late twenties / early thirties. She, too, is disorientated.

The two try independently to make sense of their new environment.

KETU discovers SOPHIE. He stares at her.

She returns his gaze for a moment.

ALEX runs onstage. He is a young man, self-assured and brash, with a childlike quality that makes him attractive and likable.

All three look at each other.

Ketu
   1 . . . 2 . . .

   ALEX turns and looks around, trying to work out where he is.

Ketu
   3 . . .

   SOPHIE looks at KETU.

   4.

Sophie (*to* ALEX)
What's he doing?

Alex
At a guess . . . counting.

Sophie
Counting what?

Alex (*looks around*)
The seats?

Ketu
5.

Alex
Apparently not.

KETU *is confused. Lost in thought for a moment.*

(*To* KETU, *helpfully.*) 6?

KETU *wheels around, seeing* ALEX *for the first time.*

Ketu
What?

Alex
Nothing. Just . . . joining in.

KETU *looks at* ALEX *as if it is* ALEX *that is mad.* KETU
examines one of the boxes. ALEX *looks around again.*

Sophie (*a realisation*)
I've been here before.

Alex
Oh?

Sophie
I think so yes. This . . . sensation . . . it's familiar.

Alex
Where exactly *is* here?

Sophie
I . . . I don't know.

SOPHIE *tries to think.*

Ketu
7.

Sophie
I wish he'd stop that!

Ketu
8.

Just then KETU *comes up to* SOPHIE. *He looks at her closely.*

Sophie
Hello.

KETU *flinches and rubs his neck.* KETU *is confused by the sensation.*

What's wrong?

Ketu
What?

Sophie
With your neck?

Ketu (*offended*)
There's nothing wrong with my neck . . . you don't like my neck . . . you don't have to look at it!

The two part. SOPHIE *slowly reaches for the top of her head.*

Sophie
I have a cut . . . here.

She traces her hand along the extensive incision.

Alex
What?

Sophie (*not wishing to pursue the thought*)
Nothing . . . it doesn't matter!

KETU *comes to a realisation, he sniffs the air.*

Ketu
There is no smell.

They all look at their surroundings.

Alex

This isn't right. This is not right at all.

They all look at each other.

Just then a voice is heard from the darkness.

Guide

Good . . . this is very encouraging. Very encouraging.

The others are startled. KETU dashes and hides behind a box. A figure enters the space. He appears to be a man in his fifties. As we shall see, he is something of a chameleon. He is able to change his physical and vocal characteristics with remarkable speed. He is the GUIDE. Though at times he appears more of a jester or a clown. Unlike the others, he appears to belong to this place.

I'm sorry to have left you alone all this time . . . there's a bit of a backlog. Well, backlog's the wrong word really . . . since time doesn't exactly . . .

Alex

Who the hell are you?

Guide

I'm coming to that . . .

The GUIDE takes centre stage.

If I could have your attention for a moment . . . I have a short presentation.

Alex

Look this is very interesting but . . . !

The GUIDE suddenly changes tone and physical character. He appears more sinister.

Guide

You have something better to do? Eh? Somewhere more important to be?!

ALEX *is chastened. Clearly he doesn't.*

Good . . . then I shall begin.

A beat.

Welcome . . . to death.

Silence.

Welcome. You will shortly be embarking on your transit. This can be a disorientating experience but we shall do all we can to make your final journey a safe and pleasant one. Please listen carefully to the instructions and follow them . . . (*Darkly.*) to the letter!

You are to select one memory from your life. You will then record your selection with the camera provided.

He points towards the 'magical' camera, an invisible device.

As the memory is captured the mechanism will flash.

There is a sudden flash. The others blink and look away for a moment.

At this time all other memory data will be deleted. If these criteria are met within the allotted timeframe, you will be united with your selected memory for living and reliving throughout eternity. Thank you for your attention.

They all look at him astonished. The GUIDE *then remembers something.*

Oh, and I encourage you to decide quickly . . . as the next group will be here very soon.

Silence.

So. Are we clear?

Alex
Clear?

Guide
Mmm . . . I thought I was clear. And rather good as a matter of fact . . . (*He preens.*) Combining an authoritative tone with an approachability that would put the listener at ease. Didn't you think?

Alex (*coldly*)
Where's the door?

Guide
The what?

Alex
Where's the fucking door?!!

Guide (*laughs in his face*)
Do you have any idea how absurd it is to threaten me?

Alex
I'm not dead.

Guide
So certain . . . Ever been dead before?

Sophie (*tentatively*)
I have . . . briefly.

ALEX *looks at* SOPHIE.

Alex
And?

A pause. SOPHIE *nods to indicate that the* GUIDE *is right.*

Oh my God.

Sophie (*to the* GUIDE)
So who are you then . . . 'Death' himself?

Guide
If it helps you . . . then yes.

SOPHIE *looks unimpressed.*

What? You expected a scythe?

KETU *is fascinated. He approaches the* GUIDE *and examines him from several angles.*

Ketu
God? Are you God?

Guide (*smiles*)
Well, that's very flattering but . . .

Ketu
The devil?

Guide
No . . .

Ketu
The wood spirit?

Guide
No, really . . . these concepts are not helpful.

Ketu (*he thinks*)
Please . . . I have so many questions . . . There's so much I need to know . . .

Guide
No! (*To all.*) This point is the culmination of your being. It's a unique opportunity that I urge you not to squander. Please . . . concentrate on the task.

A beat.

Alex
But . . . I don't even know what happened to me.
(*To* SOPHIE.) Do you?

Sophie
Yes. But I'd . . . rather not discuss it!

Alex
I'm sorry?

Sophie
I can't claim to be versed in the etiquette of this place, but I'm sure it must be impolite to discuss the manner of one's demise.

Guide (*impatiently*)
Your memory please.

Alex
Oh my god . . .

Guide
What is it?

Alex

Nia . . . My girlfriend . . . I had plans . . .

Guide (*loud*)

Plans?! There are no more plans . . . all you have is what you did!

The GUIDE *turns to* KETU.

Did you have someone? Friends . . . family?

Ketu

Of course I did!

Guide (*to* SOPHIE)

And you?

Sophie (*unwilling to be drawn on this*)

I . . . I knew lots of people.

Guide (*to all*)

If you have someone that is really important to you . . . then choose a memory with them. (*To* ALEX.) If you choose to remember her, you will always be together.

Alex

What if I choose something else?

Guide

Then she will not have existed to you. (*Very serious.*) Be sure this is *the* most important memory of your life.

Pause.

Alex

Of course I'm sure . . .

The lights slowly change.

Alex's memory

In a corridor of light that is reminiscent of a road, ALEX *and two of the other performers get into position for the start of a motorbike race.*

Alex
A race . . . there was a race. The biggest race of my life.

From the off, the voice of a mumbling FRENCH COMMENTATOR *announces the starting line-up.*

French Commentator (*off*)
Les concurrents sont sur la piste de départ, le favoris l'anglais est aujourd'hui en concurrence avec Gomez pour le titre...

Meanwhile the three racers adjust bootstraps and helmets.

Alex
And Nia's in the stands, cheering me on . . .

ALEX *waves at somebody in the stands.*

To my left, I see Gomez.

GOMEZ, ALEX's *arch-rival, snarls at him.*

The voice of the mumbling FRENCH COMMENTATOR *counts down to the start of the race, reaching fever pitch.*

French Commentator (*off*)
Cinq, quatre, trois, deux, un, et c'est parti!!!!

Alex
I wrench the throttle . . . go, go, go . . .

The performers jostle for position.

Second gear, third gear. Everything blurs. Ahead of me the heat turns the track to liquid. Pure acceleration! Everything around me disappears!

One rider falls behind and disappears.

Yeah, downshift, left turn ahead . . . turn left.

They turn left.

I'm moving up the pack. Right turn ahead . . . turn right.

They all turn to the right. Then another right. GOMEZ *catches up with* ALEX.

Someone catches up with me, I recognise the green and yellow helmet. It's Gomez!

The voice of the mumbling French commentator describes GOMEZ *catching up with* ALEX *and overtaking him.*

French Commentator (*off*)
Gomez est en train de rattraper l'anglais, oui, il le reprend dans le virage!! C'est extraordinaire ce qui se passe ici!!!

Meanwhile GOMEZ *overtakes* ALEX *and disappears.*

Alex
The long straight . . . accelerate!

Spectators at the roadside wave at ALEX.

. . . open up the throttle and fly! 120 . . . 130 . . . 140 miles per hour.

Suddenly NIA *appears on stage, an attractive woman in her thirties. She gets on the bike with* ALEX.

I feel her arms around me. She holds me so tight. That's odd.

Another right turn. GOMEZ *appears again, in front of him.*

Gotta catch Gomez!

The voice of the mumbling FRENCH COMMENTATOR *describes the ensuing battle for the lead.*

French Commentator (*off*)
Mais l'anglais reprend l'avantage!, oui, il le rattrape après la ligne droite . . . Gomez n'est plus qu'a quelques mètres, il le rattrape!!!

Meanwhile ALEX *is almost catching up with* GOMEZ.

Nia
Alex . . . please . . .

Alex
Not now baby.

NIA *slides off the bike. She talks directly to him.*

Nia

Alex, this never happened.

Alex

I can win this!

GOMEZ *overtakes and disappears. Lighting change.*

Void

Nia

This isn't real! It was just a game . . . a game we used to play. You never raced.

Alex

The bike . . .

Nia

It was your job. Monday to Friday? 9 to 5?

Alex

I was . . . a motorbike courier.

Nia

A courier . . . with a hell of an imagination. (*To the others.*) Sometimes, when we rode through London, we'd see other bikers and pretend we were in a race. (*To* ALEX.) And you and your mate Gomez used to play at being arch-rivals.

Alex

It was real to me.

Nia

So, what about me?

Alex

You were on the bike.

Nia (*flatly*)

Oh joy! I get to sit on the back of your bike for all eternity.

Alex (*he suddenly thinks*)
What the hell am I doing? I don't have to have this row!
No . . . I'm in control here . . . this is my mind!

(*To the group.*) Apart from which if I'm going to live a
moment with her for all eternity . . . I'm sure as hell not
going to pick a row!

He circles NIA, *looking at her in detail.*

This is crazy. Look at you . . . crystal clear in my mind
. . . it's like you're really here.

Nia
I *am* really here.

Ketu (*making the connection*)
Four seats, four people.

ALEX *backs off swiftly, startled and horrified.*

Alex
No . . . not you . . . not you too!

NIA *and* ALEX *embrace.*

Nia
I've had the speech.

ALEX *stares at her horrified. He rails against the* GUIDE.

There was no warning! We should have had a warning!

Guide
I'm sorry to have to say this, but frankly you're wasting
your time. Your chosen memory please.

Alex (*angry*)
Fine! When I was seventeen I had a really satisfying
bowel movement!!

Guide (*shouts*)
You want to spend eternity taking a shit . . . that's fine
with me. But I don't recommend it!! Believe me, I am
trying to help!

Sophie
How are we supposed to know? It's so difficult . . . all those years . . . to pick out one single moment?

Guide
I appreciate your difficulty . . . but you must try.

Nia
What if we choose wrongly?

Guide
All decisions are final.

Ketu
And if we don't decide?

A beat.

Guide (*darkly*)
It's . . . not an option you want to consider. There is nothing in your experience that could come close to the suffering you'd endure. (*Smiles.*) So . . .

Silence.

No one? I'm surprised. I often get people who know straight away. As if they'd thought about it at length during their lives.

He happens to look at SOPHIE.

Sophie
Why are you looking at me?

Guide
Am I?

Sophie
You know what happened to me.

Guide
I assure you I don't. And I don't need to know.

Sophie (*reassured*)
Alright. (*Thinks.*) I suppose I did . . . have the chance to reflect.

She takes a moment.

I think I'm ready.

The lights slowly change.

Sophie's memory

Sophie

I was twelve years old. My mother had guests for the evening. I was to make an appearance and I wanted to look my best.

I went into my mother's bedroom.

SOPHIE *opens the bedroom door. During this the other performers create a mirror.* SOPHIE *approaches the mirror.*

I looked at the carefully arranged tools she used to maintain her perfection.

She picks up powder.

Her powder, in a round tin, with a pattern of Bougainvillea.

As she powders her face, another performer becomes her mirror image, copying all her actions.

Her hairbrush, its handle inlayed with ivory.

She brushes her hair.

I made my lips the same deep red as my mother's.

She puts on the lipstick.

The mirror image suddenly becomes Sophie's MOTHER. The mirror disappears.

Mother

Sophie . . . what are you doing?

Sophie (*surprised*)

I was just . . .

Mother
What have you got on your face?

Sophie
I wanted to . . . look my best.

Mother (*patiently*)
Come on . . . everyone's asking where you are.

Sophie
Mother . . . tell me how I look?

Mother
How do you look? You look . . . lovely.

Sophie
Lovely? Not beautiful?

Mother (*smiles*)
Come downstairs.

The MOTHER *disappears.*

Sophie (*narration*)
I knew then I was not beautiful. Not beautiful.

Lighting change. The camera has failed to flash.

Void

Ketu
It didn't flash!

Sophie
I'm still here. (*Panicky.*) Why? I made my choice.

Nia
Why didn't it flash?

Sophie
I want to go. I want to get out of here!

Guide
Why did you choose that particular memory?

Ketu

Yes, why choose something so painful?

Sophie

Because . . . at that moment . . . I knew who I was.

Guide

Did you? Really?

Sophie

If I couldn't be beautiful I could be strong. It was a complete turning point. I decided there and then to make a success of my life no matter what.

The GUIDE *weighs this up. He is not overly impressed.*

Sophie

What? (*Angry.*) Who are you to judge me? Who do you think you are?!

Nia

Yes, who are you?

Guide

That . . . is a very good question. (*Brightly to the group.*) Now if you'd all like to think a little harder . . . I really don't want us to miss our deadline . . . (*Laughing to himself.*) Deadline!

Alex

What if we never had our greatest memory?! What if there was s'posed to be some incredibly momentous event out there in the future . . . only . . .

ALEX *stops. He is beginning to remember something.*

Nia

Alex?

Alex (*in a cold sweat*)

All this time . . . I've been thinking it was the bike . . . some stupid accident. (*A beat.*) Smoke . . . It was the smoke!

Nia (*realising*)

We were in bed, asleep.

Alex

I was dreaming that I couldn't breathe, that I was coughing. I couldn't wake up. Couldn't move at all.

Nia

A fire!

Alex

We were only staying there one night. We weren't even going to stop . . . only we were so tired!

Slight pause.

Guide

I know what you're thinking . . . what a pointless waste of precious young life. But you must understand, how you got here is irrelevant. You won't remember it after today anyway.

A pause.

Ketu

9, 10, 11 . . .

The GUIDE *approaches* KETU.

Guide

What are you doing?

Ketu

It helps me to think.

The GUIDE *is fascinated by this.*

Ketu

In my village I was known for my study. I observed things. Why did this flower have four leaves and this one ten? Why five fingers on a hand and not six?

Guide

Intriguing.

Ketu

You don't count?

Guide

I'm a little out of practice. 16, 17, 18 . . .

Alex

Oh don't you start!

Guide (*deliberately trying to annoy* ALEX)

Time is short! 19, 20 . . .

KETU *stands and speaks.*

Ketu

I have decided.

Guide

Yes!

Ketu

It is so obvious. My great revelation.

The lights slowly change.

Ketu's memory

Ketu

In the beginning the world was flat, like a plate.

The other performers transform into rainforest trees. As KETU *paddles on his canoe, the trees move towards him. Once they reach him, each in turn transforms into another traveller on a canoe. On hearing the sound of a monkey, they shoot it with a blowpipe.*

Life in my village was not easy, but the forest always provided.

The other performers engage in rural activities thus establishing the countryside.

I often found myself musing on the nature of things. Why, when I throw a stone into the river – (*He throws a stone.*) – are the ripples always circular? Why do birds choose to fly in such regular patterns?

And then one day I asked myself . . . why does the sun go down over one edge . . . and come back up on the other?

A sudden thought struck me. I took my spear and
planted it in the damp earth. (*He plants the spear.*)
I marked the spot where the sun's shadow fell . . . and
then I waited.

*KETU follows the course of the sun's shadow over a
day.*

As the day wore on I saw an unmistakable pattern
appearing.

*He picks up the spear and draws it on the ground.
An arc of 180 degrees.*

So many patterns, so many questions – I had to find the
answers. I decided to see the elders.

*KETU rushes back to the village. The performers now
take on the role of a group of ELDERS chatting.*

Why does the sun go down over one edge . . . and come
back up on the other?

The ELDERS deliberate.

Elder

Ketu . . . Why is it that your family is hungry and all you
bring home is food for thought?!

*The ELDERS continue chatting. KETU leaves. The
performers transform into a house, with kids playing
outside.*

Son

Hi daddy!

Ketu

Go inside, children.

They enter the house.

Wife

Dinner's ready!

The house transforms into a table.

Son

I'm so hungry!

They eat. The children throw an orange back and forth.
KETU watches, inspired by the arc of the orange.

Wife
Children, stop it!

Ketu (*to* WIFE)
No, wait . . . (*To* KIDS.) Go on.

Wife
Ketu?

The kids joyfully throw the orange back and forth.
KETU catches it at the height of its arc.

Ketu
You see this pattern?

He holds the orange up high.

(*Grandly.*) The world is round . . . like an orange! And
the sun rotates around it!

Lighting change. The camera has failed to flash.

Void

Alex
Is this a joke?

Ketu
What is wrong with it?

Guide
Nothing.

Ketu
But . . . this is madness. Such a discovery . . . it
changes everything.

Alex
This thing . . . whatever it is . . . it cannot be working.

Ketu
Or else it is as stupid as those fools in my village. (*To* SOPHIE.) Tell me . . . do you believe the sun rotates around the earth?

Sophie (*laughs*)
Me? Well no.

Ketu
No? (*Incredulous.*) You think the Earth is flat?

Sophie
Of course I don't. The sun is at the centre . . . everyone knows that. The Moon orbits the Earth, The Earth and the other planets orbit the sun.

Ketu
The Earth orbits the sun?

Sophie
Of course. (*Stating the obvious.*) And the Earth rotates once a day . . . ?

Ketu (*cannot fathom this*)
Impossible. The speed . . . we'd fly off into space.

SOPHIE *laughs.* ALEX *approaches.*

Alex
You been up a *tree* all your life?

Ketu
What? (*To the group.*) Do you all believe the Earth is round?

Alex (*in confirmation*)
Like an orange.

Ketu
But . . . (*He laughs.*) This is wonderful! I knew I was right. I was the only one in my village who knew the truth.

He looks at the GUIDE.

How can I have a greater memory than that?

Guide

You really think your discovery was so important.

Ketu

Yes. My people are wise but they are too attached to the old ways. I always believed there was a greater world than the one we saw. Fabulous places beyond the forest . . . where all my questions would be answered.

The GUIDE *is unimpressed with this.*

But I was right!

Guide

I'd try again if I were you.

Ketu

But . . .

Guide (*with a sense of menace*)

22, 23, 24 . . . anyone else?

KETU *backs off.*

Nia

Alex . . . Are you going to choose a memory of me?

Alex

Of course.

Nia

No hesitation?

ALEX *looks slightly confused.*

Haven't you thought about what you're losing? If I don't choose say . . . the time I finally beat my big sister at Chess . . . then I lose her forever. And my family, friends . . . everything I did.

Sophie

What about all the things I did alone? If I'm not there to remember them, they might as well never have happened.

Guide

I really must urge you to decide. Eternity won't wait forever you know.

The GUIDE *allows himself a wry smile.*

Sophie
You think this is easy?

Guide
I never said it was easy.

They stare at each other.

Nia (*to* ALEX)
I know! If we could think of a moment . . . something
fantastic that we both shared.

ALEX *is unable to concentrate.*

Guide
35, 36, 37 . . .

ALEX *shoots the* GUIDE *an angry look.*

Nia (*intervening*)
I have an idea. The day we met.

Alex
(*Recalls.*) Yes . . . of course!

Nia (*excited*)
Let's try. Yes?

ALEX *nods.*

The park. By the swings. I was babysitting my best
friend's kid.

Alex
And I was there with my nephew.

The lights slowly change.

Alex and Nia's memory

The park. NIA *pushes a child on a swing, while* ALEX *plays ball with a boy.*

Alex

I thought . . . she looks . . . interesting. But she's got a kid.

The children's movement freezes. NIA *approaches* ALEX.

Nia (*to* ALEX)
And I knew you were thinking that.

Alex (*to* NIA) How?

Nia (*to* ALEX)
'Cos of the way you looked at me . . . and . . . 'cos I was thinking the same thing.

The children 'come to life' again. NIA *returns to the swing.*

Alex

I started to run all these scenarios . . . she's a frustrated mother . . . her husband died for his country . . . or he's so boring she's looking for someone else.

Nia

And I thought . . . what's he doing . . . looking at me like that? What's his wife going to think?

Alex

Some guy walks up . . . I think . . . OK here we go . . . this'll be good ole hubby.

The children's movement freezes again. One of the performers crosses the stage.

Nia (*to* ALEX)
I didn't even see him.

Alex (*to* NIA)
He walked on past.

The children 'come to life' again.

Nia

I'm thinking . . . if I'm out with my friend's child maybe he's babysitting too.

Alex

And I'm trying to devise a way to show he's not mine. I try deliberately forgetting his name. (*Calls.*) Hey Tony . . . er . . . Timothy . . .

Nia

OK so it's not his child . . . but that doesn't make him single.

The children go into a sandbox.

And the kids start playing together.

Alex

Perfect!

Nia

Jenny, don't get dirty . . . your mother'll be here any minute now!

She gives ALEX a quick sideways glance.

Alex

Ah hah.

(*Calls to the child.*) Thomas play nice with the little girl. You're a gentleman remember?

He smiles at NIA, who smiles back.

She's definitely smiling at me . . . might as well show her I'm not wearing a ring.

ALEX *puts his hand up near his face.*

Nia

What's wrong with his face? Is he picking his nose?

She looks away.

Alex

That did the trick. She's gone all bashful on me.

Nia

OK . . . let's play this nice and cool. Let him come and talk to me.

Alex

Maybe I should let her introduce herself. This is the twenty-first century after all.

They both wait. Nothing happens.

Meanwhile the children have a great time playing together.

Nia

Now what?

Alex

Don't tell me I was wrong.

Nia

He's not waiting for me is he?

Suddenly the GIRL throws sand on the BOY's head. The BOY cries.

ALEX and NIA go into the sandbox.

Nia

Jenny, be nice to the little boy!

Alex

Thomas, it's all right. Come on, let's build a castle.

Nia

Yes, a castle! Look Jenny.

ALEX and NIA sit on the floor with the kids and start to build a sandcastle.

The kids leave unnoticed.

ALEX and NIA look up and find each other's eyes.

And at that moment.

Alex

I knew.

Nia
I knew.

Alex
I'd met 'the one'.

Nia
I was in for a wicked shag!

Lighting change.

Void

Alex
What?

Nia
What?

Alex
You were only thinking about sex.

Nia
Well, yes . . .

Alex
But . . .

Nia
Oh come on Alex . . . *you* were too . . . admit it. You couldn't possibly have known I was 'the one'.

Alex
Why not?

Nia
Because . . . People don't just *know*.

Alex (*irritated*)
Well there's no way I'm picking this memory, if you just saw me as a good shag.

Nia
Alex . . .

ALEX *turns away.* KETU *approaches him.*

Ketu

Your truth is not *her* truth. It was the same between me and my people!

When I told them of my great discovery . . . They could not see my intentions . . . that, at last, we could achieve great things. Instead they turned on me.

Sophie

I achieved great things . . . of course . . . why didn't I think of this before?

Guide

Go on.

Sophie

Oh, where to begin . . . let me see . . . yes.

The lights slowly change.

Sophie's memory

Sophie

I was twenty-one . . . It was my first day in a new job and I felt myself at the start of a great adventure.

SOPHIE *enters the office. She is greeted by her boss* MR GRAY.

Mr Gray

Sophie, bright and early I see, excellent. Go and see Jerry.

The office appears. Three desks: one downstage left (JERRY's), *one further up stage and to the right* (PHIL's) *and one upstage centre* (MR GRAY's). SOPHIE *joins* JERRY.

Sophie

It was a little daunting at first.

Jerry (*at lightning speed*)
If you're sent a B.Y.30, you input the data into one of these cells, unless it's marked 'current imperative' in which case it goes in here, but you must remember to create a separate hard copy, send a purchase order to accounts payable and cc it to me. Clear?

During this JERRY *has put his hand on* SOPHIE's *shoulder in a suggestive way. She moves away from him.*

Sophie
Crystal.

Then MR GRAY *presses his intercom button.*

Mr Gray
Phil. I could do with those Tokyo figures as soon as you have them.

Phil
Sure.

Mr Gray
And if you'd grab me a coffee I'd appreciate it.

Phil
Hey Jerry . . . two coffees please.

Jerry (*to* SOPHIE)
Three coffees please, love. Thanks.

The office dissolves.

Sophie (*narrates*)
Those first days were tough, but I was determined.
I followed my mother's advice. Meet the right people, shake the right hands, laugh in the right places and always be ready to make your move.

My chance came at the staff Christmas party.

The party appears. Champagne is popped. A bar area appears downstage left and PHIL *has made it his home. He cheerfully sings a line from 'Jingle Bells'.*

JERRY *and another colleague,* LUCY, *are upstage right.*
The atmosphere is a little stilted at this point.

Lucy
Well . . . what a year.

Jerry
Yes indeed . . . it's certainly been a year.

SOPHIE *joins them. She smiles.*

We were just saying how it's been a . . . year.

Sophie
Yes . . . absolutely.

They all smile awkwardly. The action moves over to the
bar area.

Just then the MR GRAY *shows up.*

Phil
Ah, Mr Gray, can I get you a Christmas drink.

Mr Gray
Er, large single malt scotch please.

Phil (*to the barman*)
Two large single malts please.

Mr Gray
Thank you.

Phil
My pleasure. Actually I've been looking for an opportunity
to float a couple of ideas in front of you. The thing is
I think I've figured a way to . . .

SOPHIE *approaches.*

Sophie
Sorry . . . I didn't mean to interrupt.

Mr Gray
Sophie! No, not at all, join us please.

Sophie
I just wanted to say . . . I heard your speech at the
WGB conference. It was . . . truly inspiring.

Mr Gray (*pleased*)
Really?

The action at the bar freezes. The focus switches to
LUCY *and* JERRY. *They are now a bit drunk and flirt*
with each other.

Jerry (*telling a joke*)
And he says . . . as long as it's not with citrus fruit!

Lucy
Citrus fruit!

They laugh.

Action returns to the bar area.

Sophie
. . . Truly inspiring.

Mr Gray (*grins*)
Thank you. Can I get you a drink?

Sophie
Yes, orange juice, please.

Mr Gray
Orange juice? (*He orders.*) Orange juice.

SOPHIE *smiles.* PHIL, *who has been trying to catch*
MR GRAY's *attention, gets the message.*

Phil
Perhaps we can . . . continue our chat later.

Mr Gray (*not interested*)
Mmm.

Sophie (*to* PHIL *as he goes*)
Merry Christmas.

Phil (*darkly*)
Happy New Year!

SOPHIE *joins* MR GRAY *at the bar.*

Sophie
And your point about foregrounding ethical responsibility
as a marketing tool really struck me. In fact I've been

putting in some extra hours devising ways to maximise implementation on that front.

Mr Gray (*laughs*)
Excellent!

The party dissolves.

Sophie (*narrates*)
From there it all went very quickly. Three months later I was being welcomed to the ranks of middle management.

The office appears once again. SOPHIE now occupies PHIL's old desk. PHIL is sat at the downstage desk with Jerry.

Phil (*to Jerry*)
I've got this whole plan . . . major strategy rethink . . . here's what I figured . . .

MR GRAY presses the button of the intercom.

Mr Gray
Sophie would you come into my office. I've got a couple of ideas I'd like to run by you?

SOPHIE gets up, then stops to think.

Sophie
Phil, two coffees please . . . in Mr Gray's office.

Phil (*bitter*)
Sure.

The office dissolves.

Sophie (*narrates*)
The following years marked a period of rapid growth. I was responsible for much of the company's streamlining. With an aggressive package of acquisitions we are now more strongly placed in the market than ever before. And tonight I am delighted to accept your award of Manager Of The Year!

The office has transformed into a conference centre. The other performers applaud. A PHOTOGRAPHER gets into position to take SOPHIE's photo.

Photographer

Smile!

Lighting change. The camera has failed to flash.

Void

Sophie

But . . . My success . . . Everything I'd achieved.

Guide

Were you happy?

Sophie

Oh please, I thought here at least we'd be beyond such simplistic thinking.

The GUIDE *gives her a searching stare.*

I made sacrifices. I didn't want a family . . . or a lover . . . not until I'd achieved my goal.

Ketu

What was your goal?

Sophie

Respect.

Nia

From whom?

Sophie

Everyone.

Guide

No one in particular?

The GUIDE's *manner has become that of a barrister conducting a cross-examination.*

I put it to you . . . You worked day and night . . . you rejected the advances of any men who came near you. You had no hobbies, or home life. Who were you trying to impress?

Sophie

You want me to say my mother.

Guide

Yes I do . . . and you have . . . thank you.

Sophie

But . . .

Alex

Is he right?

Sophie

My mother helped me to see what was important in life. Work hard when you're young . . . get somewhere and then enjoy your success.

Ketu

So what went wrong?

Sophie

Nothing.

Guide

Really . . . so what about . . . this?

He sticks his finger into the top of her head, where the scar is. SOPHIE *leaps away from him.*

Sophie

How dare you!!

Guide

I'm sorry . . . but this really isn't a time for self-delusion!

Sophie

It was my life . . . I did with it what I felt best.

Guide

Any regrets?

SOPHIE *is upset and angry.*

Sophie

I was a success . . . I had money and power . . . I have nothing to be ashamed of.

Guide
That's not what I asked.

Sophie
I achieved more than anyone I knew.

Guide
So what have you got? Where is it?!

SOPHIE *is fit to burst.*

Sophie
I . . . It wasn't my fault.

Guide
What wasn't?

Sophie
My illness! It wasn't my fault. Why couldn't it have
struck at some tramp . . . some non-achiever . . . why
me?

They told me how much time I had . . . It was pitifully
short . . . (*Beginning to crack.*) I could feel my mind . . .
rotting! Within a month I was a useless . . . disgusting
. . . bed-bound wretch!

They came at first . . . my so-called friends . . . when
they thought I could still be useful to them . . . But
when they found out there was no hope . . . the visits
stopped . . . just like that.

My mother kept coming of course . . . She told me how
impressed she was . . . with all that I'd achieved . . .
and how bravely I was dealing with my own death.

SOPHIE *breaks down.*

What have I achieved?

Guide (*sympathetic*)
Please . . . You must understand I'm only trying to help.

Sophie
'One day' . . . I always said to myself . . . 'One day I'll
be able to sit back and enjoy all this'. But I couldn't
stop. Even when I knew I was ill I couldn't stop working.

Pause.

Nia

In all that time, there must be a special moment . . . something you want to remember?

Sophie

It must be so easy for the two of you. I bet you have a million tender memories.

Alex

We're still here, aren't we?

Ketu

You don't have to impress us.

SOPHIE *thinks.*

Do you know why birds can fly? Because they let themselves be taken by the wind.

SOPHIE *hesitates.*

Sophie

Well . . . there *was* this time . . .

Guide

Yes.

Sophie

It's probably not important.

Ketu

Go on.

Sophie

It was strange . . . strange . . .

The lights slowly change.

Sophie's memory

Sophie

It was the beginning of a week like any other week.

The performers create a busy tube train.

Voice

Mind the closing doors.

SOPHIE *jumps on the tube. The tube starts.*

Sophie

Another week of early mornings and late nights.

Voice

The next station is Bank. On arrival the first set of doors will not open. Passengers in the first carriage please move to the rear. Please mind the gap between the train and the platform.

Doors open, passengers burst out and transform into the office.

PHIL *and* JERRY *are at their desks.* LUCY *approaches* JERRY, *noticing he has something unusual on his monitor.*

Phil

Jerry . . . send it over . . . send it over.

Jerry

OK, but you didn't get it from me, alright?

Phil

Yeah, yeah.

Lucy

Oh that is utterly gross.

JERRY *hits the send key.*

Phil

Oh whoa . . . (*He clicks his mouse.*) Enlarge . . . enlarge.

Lucy

You two are crazy . . . she'll be here in a minute.

Phil
Uh huh. (*Laughs.*) I gotta cc this to everyone.

SOPHIE *arrives at her desk. She now occupies the top desk, centre stage.*

Sophie
Good morning.

All
Morning.

SOPHIE *picks up on the atmosphere in the office.*

Sophie
What's going on?

A beat.

Phil
Jerry, I told you to stop sending me junk like this while I'm trying to work.

LUCY *giggles. The office dissolves.*

Sophie
Just an ordinary day. I worked late, got back on the tube and went home.

SOPHIE *enters her flat. She presses the button on her answer-phone.*

Mother's Voice
Sophie dear, it's mum. I know this is terribly short notice but the Smiths have invited us to dinner on Tuesday.

During this message a cat meows. She picks it up.

Sophie
Hi Stanley!

Mother's Voice
Young Ned'll be there too. He's doing so well these days, you really should . . .

SOPHIE *clicks off the message and cuddles the cat.*

Sophie

Good night.

The other performers create the bed. SOPHIE goes to bed.

Sophie (*narrates*)

That night I found I couldn't sleep. And I don't mean it took me a long time to sleep . . . I stared at the ceiling all night.

The next night was the same. I looked out of my window only to see other people staring out of their windows back at me.

Two other insomniacs appear.

London became the city that never sleeps!

And that was when I noticed . . . people had started to forget the names of things.

The other performers create the tube. SOPHIE gets on the tube.

Voice

Mind the . . . Mind the . . .

Passenger

Gap?

Voice

Mind the gap.

The office.

Sophie

I seem to have run out of . . .

Phil

Paper?

Sophie

No.

Jerry

Paperclips?

Sophie
No!

Lucy
What then?

Sophie (*struggles*)
Staples.

Jerry
What?

Sophie
Staples . . . you know . . . for stapling er . . .

Phil
Paper?

The two look at each other, this is scary.

The office transforms into the bed.

Sophie
And as darkness fell once more we dreaded the night. (*frustrated*) We tried everything . . . (*These actions are acted out.*) Hot milky drinks. That didn't work. So we tried exercise. That didn't work! We even tried counting sheep.

As they begin to count sheep, in different languages, they walk and gradually arrive in the office.

And because we had not slept we gradually lost a sense of words and then a sense of meaning altogether. The whole city had amnesia.

The office. SOPHIE looks at her colleagues.

Sophie
Who are these people? (*Trying to focus.*) Work, I'm at work.

All examine their desks.

What is my work?

Gradually the office dissolves. They can't make sense of the office equipment – it all becomes foreign to them.

What's this thing for?

The performers discover each other.

(*To colleague.*) Who are you? (*Turning to another colleague.*) Who are you?

In this moment it was as if all our successes had been wiped out, all our failures forgotten. Everything and everyone was . . . (*She searches for the right word.*) new.

The camera flashes. Blackout.

Void

A pause. SOPHIE *has disappeared. The group look around trying to see where she has gone.*

Alex
What happened?

Ketu
Where did she go?

Guide
She selected her memory.

A slight pause.

Ketu
Strange . . .

Alex
It's more than strange, it doesn't make any sense. If the whole of London suddenly suffered amnesia, we'd have heard about it.

Nia (*smiles teasingly*)
Maybe you did, only the amnesia got you?

Alex

Seriously, it can't have happened.

Nia

Unless it only happened in her head. Her illness, remember?

Ketu

The scar!

Alex

But if it was all in her mind, why did the camera flash?

Ketu

There is some subtle magic to this thing. Why that particular memory?

Guide

Why do you think?

Ketu (*realising*)

The memory . . . it helped her make an important discovery . . .

Nia

It was real to her!

Alex

What about my race then? It was real to me!

Ketu

She actually lived through her memory. Yours was just a dream.

Alex

And who are you to judge?!

Ketu

No! (*He walks up to* ALEX.) The camera . . . it's in here!

He touches ALEX's *chest.*

All look at each other.

Silence.

But . . . what about my great discovery?

Nia

How come that left you here?

Ketu

Yes. (*He thinks.*) Science . . . truth . . . fact . . . maybe these things mean nothing on their own . . . it is how we each *act* on them.

Guide

What do you mean?

Ketu

It's not what you *think*, it's what you *do* with it . . . That's what matters.

The others look at him.

(*To himself.*) What was I to do with my new knowledge?

The lights slowly change.

Ketu's memory

Ketu

The Earth is round like an orange . . .

The performers are now villagers. Ketu approaches two men who are scything crops.

The Earth is round . . . like an orange.

The reapers laugh with him. KETU moves on. He finds a woman pounding flour.

The Earth is round like an orange!

The woman gives him a frightened look. KETU moves on. He finds another villager engaged in chores.

The Earth is round like an orange!

The villager gets up and threatens KETU.

Suddenly all villagers point spears at him.

KETU is arrested and shackled to a wooden frame.

An ELDER *comes to talk to him.*

Elder

Ketu . . . You must not say these things.

Ketu

It is the truth!

Elder

Our laws are there for a reason. You are terrifying people!

Ketu

Why should they fear the truth?!

Elder

It is sedition! And you will admit it. You have until sunrise!

The ELDER *leaves.*

Ketu's WIFE *enters.*

Wife

Ketu . . . I beg you . . . you must give up what you have said. They will kill or banish you.

Ketu

But it is the truth.

Wife

What does it matter? Think of me . . . and your children.

Ketu

How can you love me if I am not true to myself?

Wife

Be true to yourself. In your own mind. Just . . . reject what you have said in public.

Ketu

I . . .

The WIFE *leaves as the* ELDER *appears again.*

Elder

Ketu . . . it's time . . . what have you to say for yourself.

A slight pause.

The WIFE *appears again.*

Ketu (*in turmoil*)
The Earth . . . is flat, like a plate!

He drops the orange.

A celebration erupts.

Elder
Welcome back!

Ketu (*narrates*)
The village erupted in celebration. The 'bad spirits'
had been banished from my mind. It seemed to me
that to persist with my ideas, would cost me too much.
I resolved to convince myself of the lie. But it would not
be easy.

*The performers are once again paddling their canoes,
as in* KETU's *previous memory.*

Hunter 1 (*watching the sunrise*)
Ah! The sun is waking up.

KETU *looks at him.*

Ketu
Why do you think the sun is such a shape?

The HUNTERS *are puzzled and intrigued.*

And yet the Earth is flat?

Hunter 1
I don't know . . . it just is. (*Joking, to other* HUNTER.)
Why are the fishes in the water?

Hunter 2
(*Laughing.*) And the monkeys in the trees?

The HUNTERS *disappear.*

Ketu (*narrates*)
My knowledge obsessed me. I needed to share it with
others . . . but they were all too frightened.

The WIFE *appears.*

Tell me, why are they so blind? The sun, the earth . . . it is so obvious.

Wife

Stop talking like this!

Ketu

But . . .

Wife

Ketu! (*Cautiously*.) Your brother is coming with the children.

The BROTHER *appears with the two children. They run to* KETU.

Son

Daddy, tell us the orange story.

Wife

No! It's not a nice story.

KETU *looks at his wife.*

Ketu

Will you deny them the truth?

Wife

To save them from danger? Yes!

Ketu

Ignorance is far more dangerous.

Wife

Ketu, tell a different story.

Ketu

This is my home.

Daughter

The orange . . . tell us about the orange.

The BROTHER *stands watching. He looks intimidating.* KETU *weighs up his options.*

Ketu

In the beginning the Earth was round, like an orange.

The BROTHER *looks at the* WIFE.

Ketu

But then a foolish ignorant god, who was not looking where he was going, trod on it and squashed it . . . flat!

Wife

Come on, children.

The WIFE *and* BROTHER *leave with the children.*

(*Narration.*) I knew then I could never live on a flat Earth. To be ridiculed and threatened and rejected. Pretending to be someone I am not.

Meanwhile, the other performers create a tree.

I will sacrifice myself. But on my own terms. Not to darkness and ignorance . . . But to truth and its pursuit . . . for my children.

KETU *approaches the tree and attaches a rope to one of its branches.*

And suddenly . . . I see it all. A moment of utter clarity. Our Earth, a perfect, beautiful orb . . . and before me . . . lies the universe.

He hangs himself.

The camera flashes.

Lighting change.

Void

KETU *has disappeared.*

Guide

Magnificent! I knew he'd come up with something interesting!

When I met you I thought you were a sexy guy . . . and maybe you'd . . . (*Quoting him.*) 'be the one'. I never actually decided you were the love of my life. (*She smiles.*) But it seems you were.

ALEX *smiles.*

Alex

I don't know what to choose. There are just too many things . . .

Nia

I know! I remember my favourite Sunday.

Alex

You have a favourite Sunday?

Nia

It was the day after the carnival.

Alex

Yes, of course . . . (*Recalling.*) I'd got very drunk . . .

Nia

Margaritas at that Salsa club . . . Shall I choose for us?

Alex

Am I going to be spending eternity with a hangover?

Nia

You were OK.

Alex (*warmly*)

OK. (*Affirmatively.*) OK, let's do it!

The lights slowly change.

Nia's memory

Nia

I remember . . . It was a Sunday afternoon in my bedroom. I was sharing with that ageing socialist and his hippy wife at the time.

ALEX *lies down.*

Alex
Yeah, and wafting up from the kitchen there's a smell of that awful mung bean broth they insist on making.

NIA *lies down.*

Nia
I open my eyes . . . it's bright out . . . we haven't left the bed all day.

Pause. A ticking clock. The atmosphere is very lazy.

Nia
Hey you . . . don't I get any of the bed? (*She pushes* ALEX *to the side.*)

Alex
It's not my fault, this thing was built for midgets.

Pause. A ticking clock.

Nia
What do you want to do today?

Alex (*enjoying being in bed*)
I'm already doing it.

NIA *gets up and crosses the room.*

Nia
Yes . . .

NIA *opens a window. We hear birdsong outside.* NIA *breathes in the fresh air, before returning to* ALEX.

Let's do absolutely nothing.

NIA *drops into* ALEX's *lap.*

Alex
Good.

Nia
Good.

A pause. The clock ticks, birds sing.

(*Narrates.*) And somewhere in the haze of that utterly lazy afternoon . . . it was all there.

Sound of heartbeat.

I can feel your heartbeat . . . and my own.

Second heartbeat joins the first.

(*Narrates.*) And then you said it so quietly . . . as if I wasn't meant to hear . . . Like it's a thought you'd accidentally said aloud.

Alex (*whispers*)
I love you.

Nia
I love you.

Sound of heartbeat.

The camera flashes. Blackout.

Void

When the lights return, NIA *has vanished.*

Alex
Where is she?

Guide
Where do you think?

Alex
I was supposed to go too!

Guide
Then why didn't you?

Alex
I . . . I don't know, I wanted to!

The GUIDE *looks at him.*

That Sunday . . . I hardly remember it.

Guide

Then choose another moment with her!

ALEX *is in torment.*

You said when you met her she was 'the one'.

Alex

She was! I wanted her to be. I wanted to feel completely overwhelmed!

Guide

But you didn't?

ALEX *struggles with the thought.*

Be honest . . . for both our sakes.

Alex

It was good, great sometimes!

Guide

But?

Alex

I just can't think of a moment that *really* . . .

Guide (*interrupts*)

Then choose a moment with somebody else . . . quickly. (*He looks around anxiously.*) 86,87,88 . . .

ALEX *struggles.*

Any moment at all!

Alex

I had a lot of good moments! OK moments! . . . Why isn't OK good enough for you?!

Guide

Why doesn't the camera flash?! Eh?! Because it is connected to your gut! Apparently OK isn't good enough! For you.

Alex

That's not true!

Silence.

What are my pathetic memories to you?

Silence.

I wanted to . . . to race bikes . . .

Silence.

Guide

Why do you think I'm still here?

Alex

I don't understand.

Guide

No . . . but I'm rather afraid you will . . . and all too soon. (*Panicky.*) Please pick something, think on it. *Want* it!

Alex

I can't! I . . .

He looks at the GUIDE *beginning to realise.*

You . . . You couldn't choose either.

The GUIDE *turns away.*

All this time I thought you were some kind of angel of death . . . but you're just like me.

The GUIDE, *for once, is lost for words.*

Is this what happens . . . if you don't choose?

Guide

This and worse . . . Without thoughts and recollections to accompany you . . . to help you know yourself . . . you're nothing!

I listened to your stories as I've listened to thousands of others . . . hoping in some way they would remind me. That some faint image of my life would return . . . something I could cling to. A second chance to decide.

From the moment I saw you there was something familiar about you. I had a feeling your memory could be the one.

(*Shouts.*) Choose!

Alex
I'm trying . . .

Guide
96 . . .

Alex
No . . .

Guide
Don't stay in the void . . . 97!

Alex (*he struggles to grasp an image*)
I can't see.

Guide
98!

Alex
Nothing! Nothing's good enough!

Guide
99!

*ALEX looks at the GUIDE. The final moments slip away.
ALEX is lost.*

(*Smiles.*) Time's up.

The GUIDE leaves the stage. ALEX is left on his own.

Guide (*off*)
Sorry to have kept you all waiting . . . there's been a bit
of a backlog . . . well backlog's the wrong word really . . .
since time doesn't exactly . . .

A pause.

(*Off.*) Welcome . . . to death!

ALEX looks around himself.

The End.

A Nick Hern Book

100 first published in Great Britain in 2003
as an original paperback by Nick Hern Books Limited,
14 Larden Road, London W3 7ST in association with
theimaginary**body**

100 © 2003 by Diene Petterle, Neil Monaghan, and
Christopher Heimann

Diene Petterle, Neil Monaghan, and Christopher Heimann
have asserted their right to be identified as the authors
of this work

Photo credit: Nevil Mountford

Cover image design: tangerine

Typeset by Country Setting, Kingsdown, Kent CT14 8ES

Printed and bound in Great Britain by Bookmarque,
Croydon, Surrey

A CIP catalogue record for this book is available from the
British Library

ISBN 185459 737 X